Golf Basics 101

A Beginner's Guide to Equipment, Terminology and Understanding Your Clubs

Larry Duncan

This book is dedicated to my dad who got me interested in golf at a young age and who I still enjoy playing with today.

Copyright Act of 1976, the scanning, uploading and electronic sharing of any part of this book without the explicit written consent or permission of the publisher constitutes unlawful piracy and the theft of intellectual property.

If you would like to use material or content from this book (other than for review purposes), prior written permission must be obtained from the publisher.

You can contact the publishing company at admin@speedypublishing.com. Thank you for not infringing on the author's rights.

Speedy Publishing LLC (c) 2014
40 E. Main St., #1156
Newark, DE 19711
www.speedypublishing.co

Ordering Information:
Quantity sales; Special discounts are available on quantity purchases by corporations, associations, and others. For details, contact the "Special Sales Department" at the address above.

This is a reprint book.

Manufactured in the United States of America

TABLE OF CONTENTS

Publisher's Notes i

Chapter 1: Introduction To Golf 1

Chapter 2: Golf's History 2

Chapter 3: Golf Terminology And Etiquette 4

Chapter 4: Golf Equipment 8

Chapter 5: Getting Ready To Play 18

Chapter 6: Golf Lessons 20

Chapter 7: Clubs 25

Chapter 8: Hitting The Ball 34

Chapter 9: Golf Software 43

Chapter 10: Golf Courses 47

Chapter 11: Golf And Zen Go Hand-In-Hand 52

Chapter 12: What Is The Ideal Golf Outing? 54

Chapter 13: Final Thoughts 56

Meet the Author 58

Publisher's Notes

Disclaimer

This publication is intended to provide helpful and informative material. It is not intended to diagnose, treat, cure, or prevent any health problem or condition, nor is intended to replace the advice of a physician. No action should be taken solely on the contents of this book. Always consult your physician or qualified health-care professional on any matters regarding your health and before adopting any suggestions in this book or drawing inferences from it.

The author and publisher specifically disclaim all responsibility for any liability, loss or risk, personal or otherwise, which is incurred as a consequence, directly or indirectly, from the use or application of any contents of this book.

Any and all product names referenced within this book are the trademarks of their respective owners. None of these owners have sponsored, authorized, endorsed, or approved this book.

Always read all information provided by the manufacturers' product labels before using their products. The author and publisher are not responsible for claims made by manufacturers.

Chapter 1: Introduction To Golf

Golf

Golf is a precision club and ball sport, in which competing players (or golfers) use many types of clubs to hit balls into a series of holes on a golf course using the fewest number of strokes.

It is one of the few ball games that do not require a standardized playing area. The game is played on a course, each of which features...

Golf has seen an incredible rise in popularity over the past few decades, and that popularity continues to grow. From the days when golf was consider the pastime of a select few old folks who walked the greens in their checked pants, the sport today has a tremendous following. It can largely be attributed to players like Tiger Woods – charismatic players who captured the attention of everyone, including those who have never picked up a golf club. Added to this is Hollywood's take with movies that have portrayed golfers as the heroes they are.

While the following has changed significantly, so has the industry. There are resorts, vacation packages and even housing developments built around incredible golf courses. Finding a great place to golf has never been easier with the number of courses growing annually and those managing the courses set to make the most of the property available. There's no way to really tell what prompted the rising popularity of the sport. But if you look at the number of young people walking the greens with parents and grandparents, and the number of schools with a golf program for its students, you'll see that it's most likely a trend that will continue for the foreseeable future.

Chapter 2: Golf's History

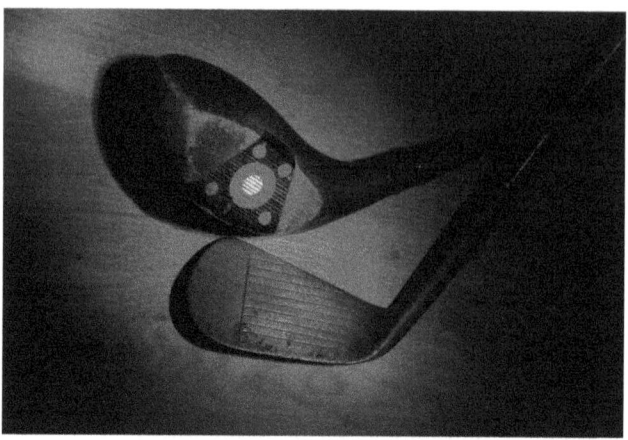

Arguably golf's interesting origin began five centuries in the past. It is a historical fact that due to the interference of golf with much more serious combat drills James II of Scotland banned golf in an act of Parliament on March 6 in the year 1457. There is general agreement among historians and golf fans alike that the Scots were the first golfers who became somewhat addicted to the sport. However, who is responsible for the invention of golf is open to debate. And debate will ensue if you breech the subject with the right people.

It has been suggested that bored sheepherders became quite exceptional at knocking round shaped stones into rabbit holes with their wooden shepherd's staffs. Making a competitive game of the boredom seemed inevitable. Various forms of golf were played as early as the fourteenth century. These games were played in Holland, Belgium, France as well as in Scotland, thus the debate of golf's origin is rightly fueled.

There is another historical fact that Scottish Baron, James VI, was the man who delivered the game we know today as golf to the English. For many years the game was played on severely rugged terrain, where no proper upkeep was required. In most accounts golf was played with crudely cut holes in the ground where the earth was reasonably flat.

It was a group of Edinburgh golfers who first formed an organized club. In 1744 the Honorable Company of Edinburgh Golfers was established. At this time in history the first thirteen laws of golf were drawn up for an annual competition. This first competition consisted of players from any part of Great Britain or Ireland.

One of the earliest golf clubs that were formed outside golf's debatable native home of Scotland was the Royal Blackheath Golf Club of England. Blackheath came into existence in 1766 and the Old Manchester Golf Club was founded on the Kersal Moor in 1818.

By the late 1800's the Royal Montreal Club and the Quebec Golf Club were to become the first in North America. It wasn't until 1888 that golf resurfaced in the United States with more fervor than each prior surfacing. Even then it was a Scotsman, John Reid, who first built a three-hole course in Yonkers New York. St. Andrews Club of Yonkers was built in a thirty-acre site near to the original three-hole course.

From the hesitant and fitful start golf grew rapidly as the new national pastime in America. Modern for its time the golf club, Shinnecock Hills was founded in 1891 and in the nine years left in that century more than one thousand prestigious golf clubs opened in North America.

The historical value of golf is as interesting as any part of our heritage. Following the path that golf took to get from a Shepherds field to the amazing golf courses that dot our culture today it is no wonder golf remains a popular pastime in all parts of the world.

Chapter 3: Golf Terminology And Etiquette

Understanding Golf Terminology

Regardless of how much you've played golf, you're probably going to hear some new terminology every time you're golfing with a new group or working with a new instructor. The way to save face is to simply nod like you know exactly what they're talking about, even when they're touting new words. The smart thing to do is ask.

Even a casual golfer knows words like bogey, slice and approach. But did you know that balata is that rubbery substance that covers a golf ball? Here are a few terms that may be less well known to some golfers.

A chunk is that boo-boo of hitting the ground behind the ball – way behind the ball. The word came about because the chunk of grass (the divot) that flies up can sometimes travel a longer distance than the ball. When it's done on purpose – as from a sand bunker – the resulting shot is called an explosion. When the ball is really buried in that sand, it's known as a fried egg.

A top shot is when you simply hit too high on the ball. One of the most common causes is that you've hit several chunks and you're trying to compensate. When you hit a top shot, the ball will have little or no loft. If you're already in a sand trap, you're likely to stay there for another shot. If there's one directly in front of you, a top shot will probably net you a fried egg.

A Mulligan is the same as a "do over" from your childhood days! This is when you aren't satisfied with your first shot and you simply pull another ball from your bag and start over. Typically, a Mulligan can only happen when you're playing alone or with very forgiving friends because few golfers are going to let an opponent have a free "do over."

Yips is a word used to denote the inability to complete a putt with a slow, steady movement. For various reasons, the golfer instead makes a sudden, jerky swing, usually causing the putt to go wild.

The address is commonly known as that moment that the golfer steps up to the ball. What some don't realize is that USGA rules say that the address has occurred once the golfer has rested the club behind the ball.

Nassau is a popular way of competing, especially for those who are something less than professional minded. In this game, golfers have one score for the first nine holes they play and a separate score for the back nine, as well as an overall score for the entire round. That means that golfers have three scores to compare, upping the odds of winning something!

There are other terms that you should know as well. The grain refers to the way the grass angles, similar to the grain of fabric. Loft is the angle of the face of the club. Dormie means that the person with the lower score can't hope for anything more than a tie.

Learning the terminology isn't necessary to playing a good game, but it probably is necessary to enjoying play with friends.

The Importance of Golf Etiquette

Even if you are not a golf pro, being on your best behavior on the course will make you shine like a true sports star. As with any sport, there are a few rules of etiquette golfers should follow.

Rule Number One:
Be on time. Most courses require tee time appointments. Make sure to arrive at the course about 30 minutes before your tee off. This will give you time to park, get your clubs, take care of cart rental and warm up.

Rule Number Two:
Obey the dress code. If you don't know the dress code, make a phone call and ask. Some courses prohibit jeans. Some forbid shorts. Some require golf shoes without spikes. If you carry a cell phone, ask if they are allowed before you hit the course. While it is easy enough to change your ringer to silent or vibrate, answering your cell phone still requires you to talk – in some cases loudly. Leave it behind if you can.

Rule Number Three:
Set an order of play before you begin. Use the old coin toss method or simply decide, but have a plan.

Rule Number Four:
Be quiet and still when a golfer in your group or in a group that is close by is preparing to hit, especially when they are putting. Don't cloud the golfer's line of vision.

Rule Number Five:
Watch where you hit! Don't swing if you run the risk of hitting a fellow golfer with an erratic ball. Likewise, don't hit until you know your ball won't drop down into the group playing in front of you. While you may think its common sense that players won't stand directly behind you when you're preparing to swing, check – just to be sure.

Rule Number Six:
Be protective. Protect the greens by replacing your divots and repairing all ball marks. Don't disturb sand traps any more than necessary and remember to rake them smooth before you leave. Here's another tip: exit a sand trap on the shallow side to avoid creating more damage to the trap.

Rule Number Seven:
Follow cart rules. If you are driving a cart, know the rules for the course. Carts may be prohibited on wet, rainy days. Some courses require carts to stay on designated paths. Always keep your cart a good distance from greens and tees and never park in another golfer's way.

Rule Number Eight:
No matter what movies or television shows portray business deals are rarely cinched on the golf course. It's not easy to talk business on the course because the game requires concentration. Don't break a golfer's concentration on the game by trying to secure a business deal.

In another matter, it is recommended that any betting on the game of golf be kept nominal, or as a "friendly" bet. Anything larger creates stress and animosity – which is far against the goal of the game.

Rule Number Nine:
Here's a tip: Tip. If you are using a caddy or assistant offered by the course, remember to tip. Ask a "regular" at the course what the norm is and tip that amount.

Rule Number Ten:
Have fun and enjoy the sport!

Chapter 4: Golf Equipment

Golf Shoes

While some kind of footwear is required on most golf courses, are golf shoes really necessary? This is a question to be answered by each individual golfer as it is his or her feet we are talking about.

Most courses require soft spikes only so the course doesn't get chewed up with the walking around people have to do when playing, especially if the people are walking the entire course. And, most club houses will only allow soft spikes to be worn inside, to protect the carpet.

Are golf shoes really needed in order for a person to play golf? No, they are not. The footwear a golfer chooses to wear is personal preference and can be practically anything from moccasins to a good athletic shoe. A golfer's footwork is more important than his or her choice in footwear.

Comfort comes first. The shoe a golfer wears should be comfortable and shouldn't pinch or cause blisters. Uncomfortable shoes will distract from the enjoyment of the golfing experience.

Because the golf swing requires a certain amount of stability, you may want to add a pair of golf shoes to your equipment list if you plan on playing regularly. Golf shoes have cleats on the bottom that allow you to maintain your footing while swinging. This can be very important as you are moving your body to hit the ball. Golf shoes help you stay balanced and keep your feet grounded.

The most important thing is for the golfer to be comfortable and confident with the shoes being worn when playing. The less a golfer thinks about shoes when playing is a good thing.

Golf Bags – A Required Investment

Few things are more important to a golfer than a good golf bag. Golf bags come in many styles and a wide variety of colors. You can choose a bag for style, features or pick a color to match your mood.

Some have legs that fold out when they are placed on the ground and stand upright so the golfer doesn't have to bend down and pick it up. That's a nice feature in golf bags, especially if the golfer tends to walk the course, as many do. There is plenty of bending to be done when a golfer is trying to remove an obstacle from around his or her ball, or to get the ball out of the cup, so any way to avoid bending over is more than appreciated.

All golf bags have compartments where the golf clubs are to be placed. Each golfer has his or her own way of doing this and putting clubs where he or she wants them. Some golfers, though, are lazy and just stick their clubs in the compartments, grabbing whichever one they want when a particular club is needed. But, some golf bags have tubes to protect the club grips. These are nice to have. With the tubes, a golfer can get his or her clubs out easier. The clubs are never tangled up, and the grips last a lot longer.

Another important factor in choosing a golf bag is the number of pockets it has. Frankly, there's no such thing as too many pockets in a golf bag. First, one of the pockets will be used to hold the golf bag's hood. The hood is used to keep the clubs and bag from getting drenched when it rains. Another pocket will be used to keep extra towels (believe it or not, extra towels are important in the summer to keep the sweat off the brow and out of the eyes, along with keeping the hands relatively dry. Then, there is the pocket used for keeping the extra golf tees and possibly the divot tool. Finally, a pocket is needed for the golf balls themselves, and it doesn't hurt to have a pocket to carry another dozen balls in, just in case.

Some courses are so difficult it is easy to lose a lot of balls during 18-holes of play. This makes having an extra box of balls around a good thing, but there has to be somewhere in the golf bag to keep them, which means another pocket.

Golf Clubs

If you think any old golf clubs will do, you haven't been on the course trying to compensate for a club that's simply too long or two short. Besides making a shambles of your golf game, ill-fitting clubs can leave your body aching after the game. If you're spending all your time compensating, you probably aren't shooting your best or even enjoying the time on the course.

Do you need to spend hundreds of extra dollars on a set of clubs with a custom fit? While custom clubs are one answer, most people can find what they need from a well-stocked golf store. But there are some things to keep in mind.

Length of the club is important, but it's not everything. The pros say that the size of your golf club's grip should be comfortable for your hands. That's why clubs for younger players and women often have a smaller grip.

If you should decide to go for a set of custom clubs, what is the process? It's nothing like be measured for a suit. The point is not only to make the club reach from the point of your outstretched hand to the ground, but also to make the most of your body – your strengths and your weaknesses.

A good custom fit will probably take place both inside and outside. The best custom fit clubs will be tailored so that your swing is taken into account. Sound expensive? Possibly.

While some major golf club manufacturers will charge (dearly) for the actual "fitting," many offer up this service for free, with your commitment to buy clubs from that company. While custom clubs are more expensive than clubs purchased "off the shelf" from your local golf store, the results will probably show themselves right away on the golf course.

Consider the shots that you may have been compensating for all your years of playing golf. If you're taller or shorter than the "typical" golfer, or even if you have some muscle strengths or weaknesses that make your game a bit more of a challenge, custom clubs can help you compensate.

Only you can decide whether custom golf clubs are a good investment for you. If you're going to spend a bundle of money for an awesome set of clubs, you may very well take the extra step to get custom clubs.

Golf Clubs for Lefty's

Let's face it the majority of the world is designed for right-handed people, with the lefties, or southpaws, virtually ignored. If a right-handed person wants to take up the game of golf, getting equipment is no problem. They can go virtually anywhere to find clubs. The same can't be said for the left-handed person who wants to play from his or her natural side.

Of course, there are those lefties who can, and do, play from the right side. This is fine for those people who can accomplish this feat. But for the majority of southpaws, the only real option is to play from the left side. (Actually, this is a misnomer as the leftie will be on the right side of the ball, while the right-handers are on the left side. Left and right, in this instance, is being used in terms of a person's dominant side.)

Most golf stores carry a selection of left-handed sets of clubs, with some left-handed putters (this is important as well, because it is as difficult to putt from the subordinate side as it is to hit from there. Basically, it does not feel natural to the player, and this will result in poor putting.)

However, should the southpaw want to upgrade individual clubs, say go from a metal shaft to a graphite shaft, he or she may have to order the club due to the lack of selection in stores. The right-hander, though, will simply be able to walk in, select the club he or she wants and leave.

Because the majority of people in the world - 90 percent at last count - are right-handed, it makes sense that golfing equipment is designed for them. But there are companies who realize the lefties of the world want and deserve quality equipment, and quality golf equipment for the left-handed player is available.

Pre-Owned Golf Clubs – An Option to Consider

If you are on a budget but golf is your sport of choice then you have many options to purchase pre-owned golf equipment. There are countless ways to own high quality low priced golf items. And even if you are not on a set income there are many opportunities to find quality golfing items that are in great condition.

Golf clubs are a very intimate part of every golf game. Purchasing used golf clubs can be tricky but not impossible. If you are patient and have an idea what type of golf clubs suit you best, resale shops are a penny-wise approach to acquiring high quality low cost golf clubs. In looking for left handed clubs or other unique features you might be surprised how easily your search for used clubs will succeed in sound results. Whether you are on a budget or just like to spend your money in a wise manner used golf clubs are a good option.

Caring For Your Golf Clubs

You and your golf clubs are going to go through a lot together: the four person benefit scramble, the company tournament and weekends of enjoyment. They become an integral part of your golf game so it makes sense to take good care of them. Golf club maintenance is easy and adds years of life to your set by simply keeping them clean.

All you will need is a bucket, some mild dish liquid (not the kind used for automatic dishwashers), an old toothbrush, and some soft towels. It helps to do the cleaning outside so you can rinse them with a water hose, but you may choose to clean them indoors if the clubs are not too dirty.

First, pour a few drops of dish liquid in the bucket. Add warm water and briskly swish your hand back and forth in the bucket to create warm, sudsy water. Don't fill the bucket too full. You want the water to cover the heads of your golf clubs, but not much else.

Put your irons into the bucket of warm, sudsy water. Use a cloth to "bathe" them. It is that simple! Once you have given the clubs a simple wash down, get the toothbrush and scrub the heads to remove dirt from the grooves.

Once you have washed your golf clubs and cleaned their grooves, you will need to rinse them. A sprayer works great so if you are outside, simply hose off the soap and dirt with the outdoor water hose. Indoors, you can simply run them under a faucet. No matter how you choose to rinse the clubs, make sure you dry them well.

Use another clean cloth and dry the clubs. Make sure it dries completely to avoid spots and damage.

Clean the handles and any wood work on the golf clubs with a dampened cloth. It is safest not to ever submerge golf club wood work into water. The water might damage the coloring, protective coat or the wood itself.

While your clubs are out, clean out your bag. A quick wipe down of the bag's interior with a damp cloth is generally all the inside needs. Follow up with a wipe down using a dry cloth. Spot clean the outside of your bag after each golf outing as needed. Once the clubs have been individually washed and dried, return them to the clean bag.

When you take good care of your golf clubs after each outing, you'll be ready to hit the greens for your next tee time!

Golf Carts

Electric golf carts can be rented at any reputable course. An electric cart speeds up the game and conveniently carries your clubs, equipment and refreshments.

If you are just starting out or on a budget, a manual golf is a good option. There are manual golf push carts and pull carts that ease the labor of moving your golf clubs both to and from the course and from one hole to the next. With prices starting around forty dollars and up, there are variations of the manual golf carts that are certain to meet the need of any golfer interested in this item.

Manual push or pull carts range in prices and features. Purchasing gently used golf carts is another way to stay geared up with quality equipment while money remains in your pocket.

Golf Balls

It is a no-brainer that golfers need to have golf balls in order to play. But, the question is, which golf balls are the best?

This is a sticky situation and will depend entirely the individual golfer and his or her tastes, what he or she expects out of the ball, and, quite frankly, how much money he or she wants to spend.

There are golfers out there who will play with nothing but one brand of ball. No matter what else happens, they will only and always use this particular brand. What these balls cost is irrelevant to them. It is this ball or no golf.

Now, let's get down to some common sense when it comes to the golf ball. The beginner needs to forget what he or she may have heard about any brand or type of golf ball, what it does and how far it goes. Beginning golfers are going to lose a lot of golf balls. They need to think more about price than quality. The beginning golfer needs to purchase "been around" balls, which are balls sold in bulk (around 50 to a bag), that have been found on golf courses and recycled, for lack of a better word.

These used golf balls are more often than not name brand balls, but this does not matter. The beginning golfer, in learning how to hit the ball straight, keep it in the fairway, out of the woods and water, will go through dozens, if not hundreds of golf balls.

Therefore, the logical thing for the beginning golfer to do is buy in bulk.

As the golfer gets better, the best idea would be to move up to a better grade of ball. This, though, does not mean to rush out to the nearest golfing supply house and buy the most expensive ball on the shelves. Again, think about the price of the ball and the level of your skill.

If a player has a tendency to slice the ball, or tends to top the ball (this is where the club head hits the top of the ball. While it gives the ball a lot of top spin, the ball does not travel far, and tends to be gashed by the club), stick with cheap balls. This does not mean stay with the bulk recycled balls, but inexpensive new ones.

In theory, players get better the more they play. As the skill level increases, the golfer can experiment with different brands of golf balls, checking to see which ones he or she may like the best. And, a lot of thought should be given to the type of course the golfer will be using these balls on.

Golf Tees

If you've never given thought to your golf tees as part of your golf equipment, now's the time to start. There are actually many types of tees that you can choose from—each with their own advantages. There are long tees when you need to have the ball teed up high, short tees for those tee box iron shots, and even three-pronged tees for stability. In fact, the three-pronged tee was the first type of golf tee that was used in the early years of golf.

Golf Gloves

A golf glove is an optional piece of equipment. The benefits of a glove are keeping the club from slipping on a hot or wet day. A glove is usually worn on the hand closest to the target. Golf gloves can be made of leather or synthetic materials. A leather glove is more expensive but it will last longer and breathe. A glove should be comfortable and fit the hand snuggly.

Golf Gadgets and Accessories

There are tons of golf gadgets and accessories out there, mainly because of the incredible increase in popularity of the sport. The more people who are ready to play the game, the more they're all looking for ways to improve their game. The result is that an industry that was doing fairly well before has boomed. There are entire companies built around a single golf gadget, and the results range from incredible golf aids to the ridiculous contraptions. Take a look at some of your options.

If you're having trouble finding time to hit the driving range and your backyard is too limited for driving practice, you have some options. You can play virtual golf, but this lacks the satisfying feel of the club striking the ball. You might find that a limited flight ball is the answer you've been looking for. These are just what the name implies. You have a ball that you place on the tee, then hit just like any other ball. But the ball won't travel outside a particular area. Or you can work with a regular ball and a net. The catch here is that you have to hit the net – every time.

Putting pads and practice aids for your putting game have been around for ages. Give yourself the advantage of practice time in your office or living room. Choose from kits that are as simple as a pad with a cup, or those that offer features such as ball return.

If you're into technology, you might find good use for a digital scorekeeper. Not only do you have an immediate way of tracking your score on the course, you have a digital record that you can save. Instantly recall scores from past games to help improve your current game.

Are you having trouble lining up the exact spot you should be aiming for on the golf ball? You can find a stencil to help. Simply use the stencil to mark the ball, place it on the tee as directed, and you've got a clear target.

How about a metronome? A golf metronome can help you work on the rhythm of your swing.

There's no doubt that the golfers have tons of gadgets to choose from. Many offer real help to the golfer, while others are simply ways to collect money for a useless product. Some of these gadgets and gizmos will be completely wasted on one golfer but will be just what another needs to improve their golf game.

Chapter 5: Getting Ready To Play

Get Warmed Up

When it's time to warm up, some golfers think they need to hit the driving range with everything they've got. In truth, warming up to make your game as effective as it can be means that you work on a variety of swings and become familiar with the conditions.

For example, you golf differently on a windy day than if the air is still. You probably play at least a bit different on days when the temperature is raging than when it's cool. Here are some tips from those who hit the courses on a regular basis.

Driving is a good way to start, but start slowly. Choose a short iron for your first few drives, giving your muscles a chance to loosen up and to get the feel for the day. Work up to longer drives, but remember that the goal isn't only to see how far the ball will go – control is more important than distance and this is your chance to gather your skills to exercise that control.

Don't just drive. Some people make the mistake of thinking they've completed an adequate warm up once they've managed to make a few successful drives. Take time for some chipping and putting as well. Make the most of your swing and any recent lessons you've had. Remember that a round of golf is much more than teeing off.

Another mistake many people make at the warm up session is to start practicing. This isn't the time to try out new clubs, new swings, or new information. This is a time to play your best game, just as you'll be doing shortly – at the first tee. It's okay to put in a few practice swings if you're working on something you want to put into play for this game, but don't get caught up in a practice session. One of the purposes of a warm up time is to build your confidence. You can't do that if you're continually making errors. Use the techniques you're most familiar with and be ready to congratulate yourself on all your successes during the warm up.

How important is a warm up? In a word – vital. The pros say this is one step that you can't afford to skip. Even if you're playing a relaxed game, golf makes some strenuous demands on your body.

If you don't play regularly, you should probably allow yourself at least a half hour to an hour to warm up before your tee time. If you play often and are in good physical condition, you may not need as much time to warm up, but you should still have some time set aside before you make your first swing.

If you neglect to properly warm up you may find yourself playing a poor game or straining muscles that simply aren't ready to be used so rigorously. Pulled muscles will not only hamper the rest of your game, it may very well put you in the clubhouse for an extended period.

Some golfers say they use the warm up time as a chance to be alone and think about the upcoming game. Others say they make a game of warming up with partners and friends. Either way, save a bit of time to get yourself ready for the game. You'll play better, both for this game and for upcoming tee times.

CHAPTER 6: GOLF LESSONS

Do You Need Golf Lessons?

If you've been thinking about taking up golf, or if you're a golfer in search of a better game, you may have considered golf lessons. But are golf lessons really beneficial? And how do you find a pro who will offer good advice?

There are some who swear that lessons are vital and others who say that practice is the only thing that will improve your golf game. The truth seems to lie somewhere in the middle. But before you drop your coach or sign up for lessons, consider what it is that you hope golf lessons will accomplish. Outlining your goals may help you decide whether you truly need lessons or simply more time on the course.

If you play with others who play exceptionally well, you may want to find someone to give you some help with your game. Whether that's a paid coach or merely a friend who plays well is strictly a personal choice. Getting some pointers and tips may be a good way to ensure that you don't totally embarrass yourself in front of other players.

If you're serious about the game, you've probably been involved long enough that you don't need advice on whether to get a coach. But if you've only recently discovered the joy of golfing, you may find yourself looking for a way to improve your game. Golf lessons could very well be the answer.

Some people say that lessons give them a set time to practice and an opportunity to completely focus on the game. You'll typically be less interrupted than if you were playing on your own, stopping to chat with friends along the way. But others say the simple fact of having someone scrutinizing every move and offering constant advice is more distracting than helpful. Decide whether you're one of those who accept direction and works well in that situation. That's a major clue as to whether golf lessons are a good idea.

Remember that a golf coach's job is to teach you to golf correctly. That means that there are some habits that he (or she) will be trying to ingrain and others they'll be trying to break. While golfing correctly is a terrific goal, many golfers have some bad habits that they tout as benefiting their game. Changing your grip, adjusting your stance or even using different equipment may be among the "must do" list from your coach. You may resist those changes. You have two options. You can do your best to follow the instructions, or you can explain that you aren't planning to change that particular habit. If you don't plan to change, you may need to reexamine your decision to take lessons. Without following directions, lessons may become a waste of time and effort on both parts, and money on yours.

Golf lessons are great for some people. It's a personal decision whether you are one of those who will benefit from a coach – formal or informal. But remember that the most important thing to improve your golf game is simply practice.

Online Golf Lessons

There are many different ways to achieve golf lessons, and many ways to effectively acquire valuable lessons. Online golf lessons are one of the fast effective ways to gain knowledge of strategies and techniques. Improving your golf game is a great reason to utilize online golf lessons.

Finding online golf lessons is relatively simple and there are many reputable websites from which to choose from. Online golf lessons can include tips on how to improve specific aspects of your golf game.

There will also be valuable information about stance, follow through of an effective swing and the finer points of swing analysis. Online golf lessons can even include time and effort geared toward the mental aspect of the game. As we know golf is a competitive sport in which you are competing against other golfer, the course and most importantly yourself.

Most online golf lessons are offered on a non-paying basis and are simply included in your favorite golf website. In some cases you may find golf lessons that are presented in acrobat reader formatting and are downloaded into your personal computer at a minimal cost to you. Shopping around to search for the most effective lessons for your level of interest in the sport of golf is of utmost importance. This will keep your costs down and provide optimal help in areas where you most need it.

Instructional Golf Videos

Instructional golf videos provide illustrated golf lessons and techniques that will improve your game. These lessons are shown in real time, slow motion and repeated as needed to insure the viewer is learning. Instructional golf videos can be purchased several different ways.

Given time anyone can improve skills at any sport. No matter if you play golf on a regular basis or are just a novice, there comes a time when what you know limits the outcome of your game. Instructional golf videos will enhance your skills both mentally and physically by providing up to date information on techniques.

Instructional golf videos are found to fit any budget and also to accommodate any degree of effective golf player. If your swing needs improving you will be able to watch golf swings as they are being analyzed. Within this in-depth view of an ordinary golf swing you will be shown the do's and don'ts for a perfectly executed golf swing.

You can find affordable high quality instructional golf videos online and in stores. These are the obvious places you can buy instructional golf videos. If you think outside of the box your local library may have media available for you to borrow.

The Online Golf Forums and Tips

When searching for ways to improve your golf game online forums and tips can be an amazing tool. From professionals to novices everyone has a reason why your golf game can be improved. And you can always have reason to improve.

With golf tips online you will experience firsthand the diversity that comes from advice given in cyberspace. You will discover on message boards and in blogs that people from every walk of life are willing to share advice and tips for golf games played all over the globe.

Many golf websites that are geared to enlighten golf fans with news and interesting facts or stories about the sport will also have links to online golf tip sites.

Time proven tips by masters of the sport will have lent you their important tips on how to survive the game of golf well under par. When you are standing on the green, waiting for your turn at the challenging ninth hole of your favorite golf course these helpful online tips will come flooding back to you and will make a huge difference in how you see the game, how you play the game and how you execute each precise effective swing.

From golf course etiquette to the finer points and semantics that rule your mental game to the demanding physical side of golf you will gain essential tips from professionals as well as from laymen.

Tips can be found online about the greatest golf courses for beginners or professionals. You can also discover through online golfing tips the cost of greens fees, the best times of the year to play certain courses and also whether or not you have the choice of nine or eighteen holes.

Chapter 7: Clubs

The One Iron

Professional golfer Lee Trevino once said not even God could hit a one-iron. This was just before Trevino was struck by lightning. He survived. And, he may be right; God might not be able to hit a one iron, though He certainly proved He could hit Lee Trevino.

A one iron is, for the most part, a useless club. It is the longest of the irons and the hardest to hit, or be consistent with. For the average golfer, or even the majority of professional golfers, a one iron simply isn't needed and just takes up room in the all-important golf bag.

In most instances where a golfer might choose to hit a one iron, a better choice would be to use a wood instead. For example, say a golfer's drive went two hundred and fifty yards on a par 4 hole, leaving him or her another two hundred and fifty yards away. Yes, a one iron could conceivably be used to hit a ball that far, but because it is so difficult to hit and control, the golfer would be better off grabbing his or her three wood out of the bag. The three wood is a good field wood and, depending on the golfer's strength, can easily be used to get the ball on the green in regulation play.

The wood is easier to hit and control than the one iron, and would be the more logical club selection in this instance.

This is not to say a one iron is good for nothing. In fact, the one iron is an excellent club to use to try and retrieve a ball lost out of bounds in high weeds.

The Five Iron

Aside from the seven-iron, the club every golfer absolutely must have, without question, is the five-iron. This is because the five-iron can be used easily, well and in a wide variety of situations.

Though not as versatile as the seven-iron, the five-iron is still a very versatile club. The angle of the club head allows the golfer to get plenty of elevation on his or her shot, while not being angled so steeply as to prevent the golfer getting a great deal of distance on his or her shot as well.

The five-iron is a great club from about two hundred yards and in. For most golfers the maximum range with their five-iron is about one hundred and eighty yards, no small distance on the links, and that is for sure. Yet, this club, this wonderful club is absolutely perfect for the distance. It allows the golfer to address the ball confidently, knowing if he or she strikes the ball properly it will hurl majestically through the heavens toward the promised land of the green.

The five-iron is also of particular use in getting out of the rough and back into the fairway, depending on how deep the rough is. If the rough is four to six inches deep, the best thing a golfer can do is grab a wedge and chip the ball back into the fairway. Sure, it will cost a stroke, but one lost stroke is better than several, and this could happen if a golfer attempted to power the ball out of the rough with their five-iron.

The five-iron is an easy club to control. Its length is just about perfect and the feel of the club is a wonder in itself. The five-iron is a marvel to swing. Why is this? This is a good question, and here is the answer. The five-iron is a mid to long range club for use two hundred yards and in, depending on how strong the golfer is and how well the golfer uses the club. Getting the reverse "C" of Arnold Palmer is a breeze with the five-iron and a golfer can generate a considerable amount of speed with the club head. The speed of the club head determines how far the ball will be hit, much like bat speed in baseball.

Because of the club's length, it is easy to control. A well hit five-iron shot will, in all likelihood, go where the golfer expects it to go, and can look like a shot seen on a televised golf tournament. It will also cover a great deal of territory in a short time, getting the golfer closer to his or her desired location, the green.

The Seven Iron

Anyone who has seen the movie "Tin Cup", starring Kevin Costner, will understand the importance of the seven iron – the perfect golf club.

A golfer can literally shoot par on just about any course using nothing more than a seven iron and a putter. Granted, driving with a seven iron will not get the golfer drives of three hundred yards, but, then again, this club was not designed to hit the ball that far. But, depending on how strong the golfer is, a good shot with a seven iron can be anywhere from one hundred and seventy five yards to two hundred and twenty five yards, and those are not distances to sneeze at.

Following the drive with the seven iron, the golfer would then make his or her approach shot. Depending on the length of the hole, the golfer will either want a full swing, or to cut their swing, thereby adjusting the distance the ball will travel. And, again depending on distance and weather conditions, the golfer may want to put the ball either in the front or back of their stance. This will give the ball more loft or keep it low, depending on which stance is taken.

As the golfer approaches the green, the seven iron can be used as a wedge to chip the ball onto the green. By closing the stance and hitting the ball in back of the stance, the golfer can flip the ball onto the green. Of course, the golfer will want to cut his or her swing or they will fly the green, which will result in a lost stroke, possibly a lost ball, and almost definitely them losing their temper.

Once the ball has been chipped onto the green, the seven iron's usefulness is pretty much over, unless the golfer has incredible courage and wants to use the seven iron as a putter. This, too, was done in "Tin Cup", but isn't advisable for the average golfer.

On short, par 3 holes, the seven iron is again the perfect club to use. Once again, the golfer can tee the ball up and hit out of the back or front of his or her stance. Depending on the length of the hole, the ball could be teed higher for more loft and less distance. Granted, it does feel awkward to have both feet in front of the golf ball, but it also prevents the golfer from getting too much of a swing and flying the green. It will, however, allow the ball to be hit higher and with more control.

And, a well hit seven iron is a thing of beauty to watch. The ball takes off in a majestic arc, following a predetermined flight plan (if properly struck), flies beautifully through the air and lands gently on the turf, bringing the golfer one step closer to his or her goal – the cup.

The 7-Wood

Of all the clubs in your golf bad, you may have overlooked the potential for the seven-wood. There are those who believe the seven-wood is the best field wood in a golfer's bag.

There are golfers who may not agree with this statement, but that's a matter of opinion. The seven-wood is as close to a perfect field wood as a golfer can have in his or her bag. This is because the seven-wood swings as easily as a six-iron, but gives the golfer more distance and accuracy.

Depending on the physical strength of a golfer, the seven-wood is a great club from about two hundred and twenty five yards in. First off, it is easy to get under the ball and get the necessary elevation to move the ball toward the green, which is where all golfers want to be in as few strokes as possible. Now, should a golfer have a seven-wood with a graphite shaft the golfer will have a better feel of the ball as compared to a metal shaft. The graphite makes the club more flexible and gives the ball a little extra lift upon impact.

Another great thing about the seven-wood is it is a near perfect club on a long par 3 or a short par 4 hole. Let's say a golfer is looking at a one hundred and eighty yard par 3. Sure, he or she could grab a three or four iron out of the bag and make the drive, and make a good drive. But, by taking the seven-wood out of the bag, the golfer has given him or herself a little something extra. He or she can tee the ball a little higher than he or she could by using an iron. This will help him or her get the ball up in the air faster and headed toward the green, especially if the drive is made with the ball slightly toward the back of the golfer's stance. This also reduces the power of the swing, so the drive won't fly the green, which is hitting the ball over the back of the green.

And, by making a slight alteration in his or her stance when the field, the seven-wood can help get around or over an obstacle. Say the golfer is about one hundred and sixty five yards out and has a tree about ten yards away, directly in front of him or her. By opening the stance a little and changing the position of the hips, the golfer can slice or hook the ball around the tree, but not have such an arc as to take the ball out of play. This type of shot still allows the golfer to get all the power he or she ordinarily would with his or her seven-wood, along with the elevation he or she expects, But without the negative consequences.

The Nine-Iron

The vast majority of golfers have a nine-iron in their bag. But many may wonder what, exactly, is this club supposed to be used for?

After all, the nine-iron can't be used if the ball is more than one hundred and thirty yards from the green. Any further back and the golfer would choose either a seven or eight-iron. And, while the nine-iron has a highly angled head, for a regular iron, it does not get the loft a golfer gets from a pitching, lofting, chipping or sand wedge, though the nine-iron does offer more distance than clubs in the wedge family.

Is the nine-iron good for anything at all? Does a golfer really need a nine-iron in the bag? The answer to both questions is yes. This is because the nine-iron is a good short-range utility club and does provide good elevation from the fairway to the green. The nine-iron can be used to chip with as well, and works well as a sand wedge should a golfer wind up in the bunker and not have a sand wedge handy.

Then again, should a golfer find him or herself one hundred and forty yards from the hole, the nine-iron can be used in place of the seven or eight iron. However, the golfer may want to think about intentionally blading the ball for the extra distance, though he or she would have to sacrifice elevation. There are times when such a shot is necessary on the course, as a seven or eight iron would be too much club for the distance in question. This will depend on the course being played and the obstacles the golfer is facing on a particular hole.

For chipping one hundred yards out or closer, the nine-iron is a good choice in clubs. By placing the ball in back of his or her stance, a golfer can get more elevation on the ball, while cutting the distance. If the golfer keeps his or her feet close together, he or she will not be able to hit the ball as hard and, therefore, will not fly the green. (Flying the green is a term used when the golfer hits a ball that carries over the green.)

In addition, the nine-iron is a good choice in clubs if the golfer is playing a short par 3 hole. Some courses have par 3 holes as short as one hundred yards, so anything more than a nine-iron will be too much club. Again, though, stance is important as the golfer does not want to drive the ball over the green. A closed stance, in this instance will help the golfer cut the distance the ball travels, while putting the ball back in his or her stance will help the ball get in the air faster. Properly struck, the ball should fly in a perfect parabolic curve, landing gently on the green with the ball, hopefully, rolling close to, if not into the cup.

So, to answer the question, a nine-iron is a good club to have around.

Drivers

In golf, the driver is also known as the 1 wood. Normally it's the longest club in the bag and has the largest head. This club is used to hit the ball off the tee out of the box, which is where the ball is teed up to start playing a hole. Of course, on a short par 3 hole, the driver would be left in the bag, and another club would be selected, unless the golfer just had a hankering to fly the green and blow any chance at making a birdie or par.

A is a great way to get the ball down the links on the golf course. A well hit ball can travel more than three hundred yards. However, this kind of driving power is most often seen on the Professional Golf Association (PGA) tour. The average golfer is doing well to hit the ball two hundred and fifty to two hundred and seventy five yards off the tee and these are not drives to be ashamed of.

There is no set average distance for holes on the golf course, which makes driving on different courses a major challenge, in some cases. Some par 4 holes can be as short as two hundred and eighty five yards, while others can be closer to five hundred yards in length. Either way, a well hit drive is required to do well in the game of golf.

The basic idea of driving the golf ball is to keep the ball in the fairway, out of the rough, avoiding sand traps, and most definitely staying away from any water hazards the course may have to offer.

The Sand and Pitching Wedges

There are several types of wedges in the world of golf. You'll likely find several wedges in your own golf bag. For our purposes today, the topic of wedges will be limited to the pitching wedge and the sand wedge.

First, wedges have shorter handles and other clubs in the bag. This is because the golfer has to get closer to the ball in order to get the elevation he or she needs to make the shot. Wedges, especially the pitching wedge, are for short shots, usually no further than one hundred yards.

The primary use for a pitching wedge is to get the ball up in the air quickly. Distance is not as important as elevation, at least initially, but the golfer does want the shot he or she made with the pitching wedge to reach the green, preferably with the ball rolling close to the cup.

The sand wedge is primarily, though not exclusively, used to get golf balls out of sand traps, especially if the sand trap is close to the hole. Because of the angle of the club's head, the pitching wedge is for extremely short distances, say within fifty yards of the green. This club is designed to get the ball in the air in a hurry, but not to get the ball very far down the course. There are other clubs for that purpose.

The sand wedge, though, can be used to get a ball out of a tricky situation. Because of the angle of its loft, approximately seventy-five degrees if properly struck, a golfer can get the ball over trees and back onto the fairway. However, if the golfer in question blades the ball, all bets are off. Blading the ball is when a golfer does not get under the ball, but hits closer toward the middle of the ball. While the ball will get in the air, it will not go very high, and it will most definitely go further than the golfer intended. However, this is the same for all clubs, not just wedges. With the wedge, though, blading is more noticeable as the ball will fly the green, costing the golfer a shot.

The pitching wedge and the sand wedge can be used in the place of a chipping wedge, yet another in the family of wedges. Chipping is done when the approach shot is close to the green, but doesn't make it onto the green. Chipping can be done when the ball is as far out as one hundred yards, though this is a more difficult type of chip and the golfer may want to consider a different club altogether.

To use the sand wedge in the place of a pitching wedge, the ball should be fairly close to the green, say, within twenty five yards. This is because the shot should be softer, more for loft than distance, and with the angle of the sand wedge's club head, it is easy to get under the ball too much and get virtually no distance on the shot.

To use the pitching wedge to chip with is easier, as the club head on the pitching wedge is not as angled. Foot placement is important here, as the golfer must decide if he or she wants more loft than distance.

Chapter 8: Hitting The Ball

Hitting a Golf Ball

A golf outsider watches the game. How hard can it be to hit a stationary ball? After all, major league baseball players hit balls traveling high speeds all the time. With that in mind, the outsider decides to take up the game of golf with the notion that the game is so relaxing because it requires little effort.

Think again.

Most of those people give up on the game before they really understand the dynamics of hitting that little ball. It makes sense that an iron club could pelt a little ball hundreds of yards, yet when the new golfer takes his first swing there is often little movement at all… sometimes no movement (or worse, backward movement).

There is a lot more to hitting that little ball than meets the eye.

Human nature is to use the iron to cup it under the ball to hit the ball up into the air. But look at the club. It is angled back, not at all designed to cup beneath the ball. So, when a golfer tries to scoop up the ball, he or she is really trapping it between the angled face of the club and the ground. That's why often times, the ball doesn't move – or worse, moves backwards just a little bit.

Instead of striving to hit up, it's best to learn to hit downward. By hitting down, the angled club will do the work for you, not the upswing of your club. When you hit down, the angle will bump your golf ball forward. It's that simple.

But putting power behind that little punt takes some practice. You'll be tempted to swing big and hard. It takes as much practice to resist that temptation as it does to learn to hit the ball! Once you have trained yourself against swinging upward, you will see your hitting start to improve.

Now you'll begin to understand why there are various golf club options and choices you have to make when making a shot. You'll need to pick your club based on the angle of the club face once you determine how far you want the ball to go and how you need it to perform.

The biggest key to hitting the ball is practice. Just as it takes a while to train your mind to think about hitting downward instead of upward, it takes a while to train your body to actually do it the way you have in mind. Don't give up and remember, the game is all about relaxing so don't stress too much over hitting the ball.

The Perfect Grip

It's easy to say that those who don't have a good grip won't have a good game. And it's easy to say that a good grip is vital to a good swing. But what constitutes a "good grip?" How do you achieve it? And if you don't have one, where do you get it?

Unlike the latest gadget, the training aid that helped you stop that awful slice or even your lucky golf sweater, you can't find a perfect golf grip at your favorite golf store. And even more confusing, if you ask any fifty golfers–amateurs or professionals–to demonstrate The Perfect Grip, you'd likely get fifty slightly different demonstrations.

It comes to a variety of factors. Unfortunately for some (and fortunately for others), golf isn't an exact science. You can't put an equation on your golf grip. But there are some things you can do to make your grip better. Take a look at some of the tips offered by the pros.

Make sure the grip on your club is right for you. Most people understand the role clubs play in a great round of golf. If you're not playing with your own clubs, you may find yourself playing a poor game of golf. But some people think that a new set of golf clubs are a wonderful gift without stopping to consider that the clubs may not fit the player. Just as a single pair of gloves wouldn't fit every golfer, golf grips are made for the individual. Take time to find what fits you best and don't settle for something else.

Comfort is another point. No matter which golf grip you prefer, you have to be comfortable with it. If you're spending all your time chanting a mantra – "right hand like so, left thumb goes here, push the left hand to here" – you can't think about anything else. While most golfers do have to spend some time practicing the grip, it shouldn't become the most time-consuming point of learning (or playing) the game.

If you aren't happy, try something new. If your grip is not comfortable or the grip on your clubs too large, fix it. Unless you're working with a professional coach who refuses to let you make any adjustments, take a look at your methods and your equipment.

If you do have someone pointing out a better method (and if your game is indicating that you need that help), take time to give it a good try. Any change in your grip is probably going to result in at least some minor discomfort. Your body, arms and hands are accustomed to working in one particular movement and a change in your grip is going to mean that all those parts have to make some adjustments. That change probably isn't going to happen naturally in just a few minutes (or hours) of practice. Give the new grip a chance to become more natural and see if it helps. It's never too late to revert, but you should at least give it a proper chance.

Your Golf Stance

Start with your feet placed just so, your body turned slightly to the left, your ball directly under the logo on your shirt, carefully line your body so that it's shaped like this, etc. And the list of golf stance instructions goes on. In fact, some people get so caught up in the stance that they lose sight of the real purpose – a perfect golf game. Defining your perfect golf game is probably more important than the perfect stance. And if you're out to enjoy the game, getting caught up in the details can really be a problem.

So does that mean that you shouldn't work on your stance? Absolutely not. The pros say the stance and swing are at the heart of a successful golf game. You may very well be able to make a great drive from something less than a great stance, but perfecting your stance will allow you to play a more consistent game of golf.

Start by relaxing. This step may take some work, especially at first when you're trying to remember the myriad of rules that make a successful stance. Your arms, though fixed in position, should never be rigid. In fact, most pros and coaches say you should start with your arms relaxed at your sides.

The actually stance depends on several factors, including (according to many) gender. There's at least a general consensus that women need a wider stance than men. Remember that your golf stance is the basis of the entire swing and that balance is crucial. Add to that the fact that the hips and pelvis of men and women are naturally different and you'll get a basic understanding of why women often need a wider stance. Because the male golfer's hips tend to be more rigid than of their female counterparts, his body reacts to the counter swing and the follow-through differently. A woman's hips are made to swing more easily and this can be a real advantage on the stance, as long as the woman compensates for that difference. Finding a comfortable standing position will likely take some trial and error, and some practice.

Finding the comfort zone is important, but you may need to be willing to compromise comfort in order to work on your stance. While you shouldn't be standing in a position that makes your body hurt, you may very well experience some discomfort while your body is adjusting to the position of a new or adjusted stance. Remember to loosen muscles before you hit the course, and to practice for short periods during that adjustment phase.

The stance is only one part of the successful golf game, but it's very important. Coupled with the grip and other aspects of the swing, it makes up the ability to play a consistent game of golf. But before you get lost in the details of the stance, remember that golf for most people is meant to be fun. If the details of the stance are killing your enjoyment of the game, it might be time to take a good look at your definition of a successful game of golf.

Golfing in the Wind

Weather conditions play an important part in golf, and none more so than wind. While a wet golf course will prevent the ball from rolling as far after being hit, and can make it tough to get the ball in the air to begin with, the wind will have more bearing on the outcome of a round of golf than anything.

Why is this? Well, first the wind will affect the trajectory of the ball, taking it out of its intended course of flight, and dropping it somewhere the golfer did not intend for it to go.

Now, let us remember the majority of golfers, both men and women, are right handed or play right handed. The wind will be discussed from the right handed person's perspective. But, first, the golfer must be aware of which way the wind is blowing, even if he or she has no idea of how strong it is blowing. Of course, if a gale force wind is blowing on the golf course it really will not matter much how a golfer tries to hit the ball, unless the wind is behind his or her back. In such an event the golfer would want to get the ball higher and let the wind do most of the work, especially on a drive.

OK, so the golfer is in the tee box, the wind is brisk, blowing from right to left. He or she is looking at a par 3 hole about one hundred and fifty yards from the tee box to the hole. The flag is in the middle of the green. What can be expected? If the golfer attempts to hit the ball directly at the flag, he or she will be disappointed to see the ball being blown off to the left of the hole. Depending on the slope of the green, this can result in the ball rolling completely off the green, requiring a chip shot to try and save par. The smart golfer would take the wind into account and plan his or her shot accordingly.

Suppose the golfer is teeing off on a three hundred and eighty seven yard par 4 hole with a stiff wind blowing directly in their face. The smart thing to do would be for the golfer to alter his or her stance to keep the ball down low and out of the wind. By doing this, the golfer can get a decent drive. The golfer must also take the wind into account on the approach shot, again setting up in his or her stance to keep the ball low. And, it would also be a good idea for the golfer to pick a club one bigger than he or she normally would. So, if the golfer would use a seven iron to cover the last one hundred and fifty yards, with a stiff wind in his or her face, he or she should consider using a five or six iron.

The Art of Putting

Many golfers spend an extraordinary amount of time learning to make an awesome drive. In truth, there's nothing prettier than the golf ball flying through the air and bouncing neatly onto the green – except the ball dropping neatly into the cup. While working on those longer shots is important, poor putting skill can literally lose the game.

Learning to put accurately every time can be a great expenditure of your time. Consistently getting to the green isn't going to do you a lot of good unless you're able to drop the ball once you're there. Take a few tips from the pros regarding the successful putt.

The "yips" are the bane of many golfers on the putt. This is simply a hesitation – rather like a hiccup – that causes you to get a less-than-smooth putt. A smooth stroke will always lend you better control over the ball.

When you're practicing your putt, pay attention to accuracy. If you're having trouble controlling the line of travel, give yourself some help until you get a better feel for the game. You might find it helpful to make a mark on your club to clearly indicate the center of the putter. Marking the ball may also help you make a very solid swing. Chalk is a good way to make these marks, because it will easily wipe off after your practice session.

Try making yourself a mental picture of the pathway the ball should travel. If that mental picture doesn't help, try laying a piece of string along the ground between your ball and the cup. It may seem like a very simple thing, but watching the point that your ball veers can help you figure out what to do to correct the problem.

Too much spin on the putt can create some problems as well. Spin is one of the most difficult things to control, and the short distance at the putt is all about control.

If it's a long putt, resist the urge to put too much muscle into the swing. Avoid unnecessary loft. The higher your ball travels, the less control you have over it.

You also have to resist the urge to overshoot your target. Overshooting is a problem in many sports – not just golf. Imagine the number of times you've seen someone take a shot at a pool table only to have the ball ricochet off the back of the pocket and bounce back out. The same sometimes happens with baseball, football and basketball when the person throwing oversteps the amount of power needed to make a successful play. It's human nature to overthrow. Guard against that at the putt. There's little more frustrating than to walk past the cup to the new putting position which is even farther from the cup than the last – all because your swing was simply too powerful and the ball passed over the top of the cup.

When you're ready to putt, take a moment and take control before you take the swing. Remember that the control is every bit as important as your aim.

The Golf Traps

It's a nightmare – You're golfing along with a perfect swing, perfect stance and you've even managed to eliminate that slice that's plagued you. Despite doing everything right, even the best golfer will find himself (or herself) occasionally mired in the sand, knee-deep in grass or standing behind the largest tree on the golf course. If golf courses were all perfectly smooth with no bunkers, sand or water, the game would likely become boring for even the most dedicated golfer. Obstacles make golf a better game, and you'll be even more appreciative of these traps if you know the best ways to get out of the situations.

What are the odds that your golf ball will roll to a stop directly behind a tree? You have a couple of options. You can bore a hole through the tree large enough for your ball to pass through, but that's probably not going to meet the approval of either your fellow golfers or the course maintenance crew.

The option many golfers take is to sacrifice one putt to put the golf ball in a better position. Whether this is your best option depends on your ability as a golfer, and how much you're willing to risk on this one play.

Sand presents another problem altogether. Many golfers choose the "whack and see" method. Just pull a sand wedge from the golf bag, whack the general area of the ball, then watch the sand flying through the air to see if a golf ball happened to take flight as well.

Consistency is the key to golfing overall, and getting out of the sand trap is no exception. Sand is a real problem when trying to control a golf ball. Golf balls don't roll well in sand and you're going to have trouble controlling a putt from the sand trap. Add to that the fact that you're often going to be dealing with an upward face of the trap before you're back on open course, and the only consistently reliable way to get out of a sand trap is to use the wedge and get enough loft on the ball to clear the face of the trap.

Choose your wedge carefully. Remember that you're looking for enough loft to clear the sand, but less loft is usually easier to control.

Regardless of the obstacle you're facing, controlling the ball, choosing the best club and setting up your shot are the steps that will get you back onto open ground.

Chapter 9: Golf Software

Learning how to play golf is definitely a "hands on" process. However, there are other ways of learning golf that will actually enhance your understanding of the game and its addictive components as well as improve your physical skills. Software that teaches an individual to play golf is a valuable resource in the quest for perfected golf skills. You may be surprised exactly how much knowledge, expertise and understanding you can gather just from golf learning software.

The instructional golf software that explains various golf lessons and is available to the general public may easily be the exact same lessons that professionals value also. Easy to follow techniques are explained and presented in unique formatting so that no one could misunderstand them. Different levels of instruction and varying degrees of cost are two diverse ways learning golf by means of software can accommodate any level of golf enthusiast.

A very important key factor to any type of instructional golf software is discovering just how effective it has been. Your favorite golfing website will have pro's and con's guides to various instructional software. Golf websites should also have direct links to free trial downloads for different golf learning software. With free trial offers you can dabble in the world of software instructions and evaluate whether a certain product would benefit your needs.

Some of the most recent technological advances have been applied to instructional golf software. Improving your golf game is the entire reason to experience the latest software available, however there are many older versions of reliable software that may suit your needs completely. As golf can be a tremendously relaxing sport it is also a competitive sport and to achieve your best swing, your accurate puts and the best score you have ever dreamed of having most of us have to endure at least a few lessons.

There are natural golfers, as well as there are some natural football players. Sport participants that shine at what they do with minimal guidance area rarity. Unfortunately most of us need not only instruction but also time and effort to gain a sense of the game. Gaining a sense of the game has nothing to do with actually becoming proficient at playing golf so with the help of golf learning software you can learn what your best is in no time.

Golf tends to be just as much a game against your-self as against an opponent. You face individual goals as well as attempting to outscore your golf mates. Software that encapsulates all the methods and techniques that need to be a focal point on any golf course worldwide is a great tool to have in your arsenal. Finding the right software for your needs is simple.

Golf Swing Analysis Software for Perfecting Your Game

When it comes to perfecting your golf game the style and technique of your swing may be the single most important aspect on which to focus. There are many instructional videos and software available to the general public that aid in perfecting a golf swing. Whether you are an amateur or a professional you can benefit from having your golf swing technique and style analyzed.

After all, one main key to a successful golf game is your swing. The key to perfecting your swing is by analyzing your technique and style. Golf swing analysis can be achieved with the newest software available or with software that has been around and been proven time and again to create a better swing in all shapes and sizes of golfers.

Whether you are a serious die-hard golfer or a recreational weekend-warrior-type golfer there is golf swing analysis software that will help you discover where your swing might be going wrong. More importantly you will learn how to improve your swing so that your fullest potential will be met on the golf course.

Some software available will have instructions from your favorite golf professionals. Other software will use every day golfers who are as eager as you to perfect their golf swing creating a notable difference in anyone's golf game in a matter of weeks.

Software that improves golf swings with analysis information is user friendly in most cases and can even be found available as downloads. Free trials are frequently advertised, making the search for the perfect swing improvement tools easier to find.

Some of the incredible tools for imaging swings and readying those images for analysis are slow motion cameras and virtual comparison software. There is golf swing help for any caliber of golf participant and there is also software available for any budget.

Golf has gained in popularity in the last decade. This interest has grown due to the phenomenal participants in the public eye. Whether you have recently become a true fan of the sport or have always been a die-hard golf fanatic, if you are ready to improve your golf swing, the latest technology software is the way to go.

Computer Software to Track Your Golf Handicap

If you're a professional golfer, you've probably got a well-documented handicap. Everyone's interested in your ability so everyone is keeping track. But for golfers who are something less than pros, your handicap may be a tedious piece of paperwork. Why not turn to technology to help?

There are several software and Internet programs available that will help you come up with your numerical handicap, and even help you track your scores to establish your handicap for tournaments.

You have options in these programs that range from online sources to purchased software packages. Prices also vary significantly and you can spend as little as $10-$12, or more than $100.

The extent of the programs varies as much as the price. You can find programs that do all the calculations for you, offering up a spreadsheet with all your stats, or choose a simpler program that merely gives you a numerical handicap.

Whatever you choose, keep in mind that your program and your figures is still only as good as your record-keeping practices. If you're one of those people who can't seem to find time for mundane tasks, you may find that you're also not able to get all the stats entered to track your handicap. On the other hand, having a computer program for the golf handicap tracking may be just the motivation you need to keep better records.

One advantage of an online service over software is that you can stop and enter the information from any device with internet access. That means that you can immediately enter your stats after your game from your smartphone or tablet. You can also print out your records from any location.

There are many benefits to establishing and tracking your handicap. While the casual golfer may have little need of a regularly updated handicap, there's no doubt that tracking your handicap can often be the incentive needed to improve your game. While making better shots on the course is a good sign that your game is improving, there's nothing like a solid number to prove the fact.

Chapter 10: Golf Courses

What Makes a Golf Course Good?

A question plaguing designers of golf courses all over the world is what makes a good golf course? The answer, simplified greatly, is the lay of the land it is being built on.

A good golf course needs to have rolling hills, preferably a pond or two, or three, or four, or five, trees, an area that can be used as a fairway, an area for a rough, and enough room for sand traps. However, there are a lot of so-called golfers who don't think a course should have any sand traps at all. They are wrong and the minority. Sand traps can improve both the course and the skills of the golfers who play them.

A good golf course should be designed so as every hole is different and unique unto itself. If every hole was straight and four hundred and twenty yards, the course would be boring to play. A good golf course should have holes that dogleg right and dogleg left, with enough obstacles so the flag cannot be seen from the tee box.

Good golf courses have elevated tee boxes to help the golfers get more elevation on their drives. Once the ball hits the fairway, the elevation will depend entirely on the skill of the golfer.

Another thing that makes a good golf course is the people who work to maintain it. Some courses have professional groundskeepers who have the job of keeping the fairways smooth, the roughs rough and the greens closely cropped. This can make the all the difference in the world to golfers, as can the type of grass used on the green.

Speaking of grass on the green, the better golf courses have bent grass greens. This helps keep the ball from rolling off the green once it hits, whereas a green with Bermuda grass, while still a good green, will not have ability to slow the ball down once it hits. Of course, the bent grass greens will wind up with more divots than those with Bermuda grass as the ground tends to be softer beneath them.

The attitude of the grounds crew and the personnel in the clubhouse has a great deal to do with whether a golf course is good or not. If the people working there are indifferent and have bad attitudes, it can affect how you view the course. A helpful, friendly staff, will make the golfing experience pleasant and enjoyable.

Well maintained golf cart paths are also important to having a good golf course. A broken and rough cart path will beat the golfers to death, forcing them to drive on the fairways. While this is not a major problem, it can be a headache.

One of the things that makes a poor golf course, is rough terrain. Rough terrain and rocks has a negative effect on the balls once they hit the ground and damages the player's golf clubs.

Same Course, New Game Every Time

One thing every golfer will agree on is no golf course is ever the same. While playing different courses is fun and challenging, playing at one's home course, no matter how many times it is done, is always going to be different.

Yes, it is the same course, nothing has been changed, except for the position of the cup on the green, but no golf course is ever exactly the same two days in a row, or, for that matter, the same day.

Will Smith in the movie "The Legend of Bagger Vance" told his protégé how the grass follows the sun, which means a putt that broke one way in the morning will break in the opposite direction in the afternoon.

Another thing that makes the same course different every day is the weather conditions. Weather plays a big factor in golf, and how a course plays. A wet course will play slower and the ball will not travel as far after hitting the ground. On a dry course, the ball will roll farther after hitting the turf.

A course will also play differently in hot or cold weather. Colder weather keeps the ball from traveling as far, while a well hit ball will go further on a warm or hot day. Additionally, if an area has been dry for any length of time, the fairways, unless they are watered heavily every day, will become as hard as concrete and provide extra distance once the ball hits the ground.

The attitude and frame of mind a golfer is in will have a direct effect on how well he or she plays and reacts to the course. Golf is a game requiring a calm, focused mind, so the player can concentrate on what he or she is trying to do on any particular shot.

One other thing that will make the same course play differently is how the grounds are kept. If the fairway is allowed to grow a little long, balls will not be able to roll as far, whereas, if they are kept trimmed close to the ground, the ball will roll further.

The rough is a whole other problem, as are other obstacles on the course, such as sprinkler heads. The rough is always going to be thick and hard to play out of, but a heavy, wet rough makes it almost impossible for a golfer to do much more than simply attempt to chip back onto the fairway. Sprinkler heads, which are positioned all over the course, will have an adverse effect on a ball that happens to hit them.

Believe it or not, who a person is playing with, or if he or she is playing alone when he or she normally plays with someone else will affect the way the course is played. So, this only goes to show how the same course, no matter how many times a person plays it, is never the same course twice.

Stimp Meters – How Fast Is Your Course?

If you are fairly new to golfing, you might not have even heard of a stimp meter yet. The average leisurely golfer might not ever need to know what a stimp meter is. But, since a stimp meter is important to the speed of a golf course, it doesn't hurt to know a little about it.

If you play golf for any length of time, you will hear serious golfers talk about how the course is "stimping." This refers to how fast the courses are running and that speed can actually be estimated with a stimp meter.

A stimp meter is the device used to measure the speed of the greens. To get the stimp rating, a ball is rolled down a little ramp (the stimp meter) in eight different directions. The stimp rating is the average distance the ball rolls once it touches the greens. For instance, a course with a stimp rating of 12 is a course in which the ball rolled an average of 12 feet once it hit the greens. Most Professional Golfers Association courses run at a 10 to 12 stimp rating. The higher the number, the faster the course. Most municipal golf courses have an average stimp reading range from 7 to 10.

Why is it important to know a course's stimp rating? You probably won't ever care about it unless you play competitively (or play with other people who play competitively). A stimp rating might explain why you've had a "bad" day on the course. For instance, when you usually score well on a course with an average stimp rating, you might not score as well on a course with a higher rating and faster course.

Another consideration in measuring stimp rate is the turf on which you are playing golf. It was once true that the rate difference was obvious between natural grass and artificial turf. Today, however, manufacturers take their artificial grass seriously. Many brands have developed special "natural bend" features that mimic the way real grass moves. There should be no discernable difference in the stimp meter reading these days on courses with artificial greens.

For golfers who like to practice putting at home, you can buy outdoor synthetic turf putting greens for your backyard. If you'd like to practice based on the course you will soon be playing, you can adjust the stimp rating on your practice greens to match that of the course you will soon play. As with any purchase, research the companies that sell such products, learn all the pros and cons of the practice turf and ask all relevant questions before you buy a system.

If the course doesn't have to travel particularly fast for you and you are content to get the exercise and relaxation that a day of golfing provides, you'll probably never need to know the stimp rating of the courses you play. But, if someone comes up to you and asks how the greens are stimping, you'll know what they're talking about.

Chapter 11: Golf And Zen Go Hand-In-Hand

Good golfers center themselves before each and every shot. While it may look effortless, there is a great deal going on. Remember the scene in "The Legend of Bagger Vance" where Bobby Jones steps up to the ball preparing to tee off. Will Smith tells Matt Damon to watch Jones's eyes, and how he sees the field. The eyes go soft as Jones takes his practice swings, getting his mind and body in tune with one another. His drive is as nearly perfect as a drive can be.

It may seem a bit farfetched, and some will object to the statement, for many will recognize the truth of this statement - Golf is a Zen experience. This is especially for the better golfers, no matter how they may joke around and seem to be goofing off.

This is what Zen is – being completely and totally in each and every moment at all times. Some people call it living life to its fullest, but that is something entirely different. Zen is more like experiencing every moment of life to its fullest and appreciating the moments for what they are.

Golf and Zen coincide on all aspects of the game. By being in the moment a golfer takes notice of everything around himself or herself. He or she notes the feel of the breeze as it is blowing across the course, recognizing its force and direction, but not actively thinking about it. He or she also notices the feel of the grass as they walk down the fairway, but he or she is not thinking about the next shot, not yet. Thinking about the shot will occur when the player gets to the ball.

At this time the player will note the distance from where he or she is to the green, the weather conditions and select a club. Avoiding distractions, the player will focus on how to make the next shot, again, though, without really thinking about it. Too much thought fouls up the mental processes causing the player to get tense and screw up the shot. Instead, the Zen golfer will trust his or her body, knowing the body and mind are in tune with one another and make the shot. For the record, not every shot will not be perfect going exactly where and how far the golfer intended. But, the major difference is the golfer familiar with, and practicing Zen, will not be adversely affected by a miss hit shot, whereas a golfer who stresses over every shot will.

The non-Zen golfer will get down on themselves, thinking how they are a lousy golfer and shouldn't be on the course at all. The negative thoughts will be invasive throughout this player's entire body as the body and mind are at odds with one another instead of being in a state of harmony. So, the end result is one bad shot is followed by another, and a good shot is looked upon as an accident, luck or a fluke.

Chapter 12: What Is The Ideal Golf Outing?

What is the ideal golfing outing? Frankly, it will be different for everybody, and not necessarily the same for every individual.

For some golfers the ideal outing would be going to a major course and getting to play on it, knowing professional golfers had played over this same course. What golfer would not want to play the course where the Master's or U.S. Open is held? Most would almost kill (figuratively speaking) for the chance. These are courses where legends have played - players such as Arnold Palmer and Tiger Woods. (Yes, Woods can be considered a legend of golf based simply on the fact he has won so many tournaments at such a young age.)

For others, ideal golfing is not so much where they play as to the weather conditions. Some golfers prefer a day with mild temperatures and a light breeze to help keep them cool, while others want a challenge and will go to the extremes weather-wise. There are those who will play when the temperature hits triple digits, or drops well below freezing, just to see how well they play under these circumstances.

For most golfers, though, the ideal golf outing is simply the chance to go to their favorite course with a few friends and chase golf balls all over the pasture, just having a good time and not take the game too seriously. This is the most prevalent type of golfer, and these players can usually be found playing in couples and foursomes. They will chide one another on a bad shot, while complimenting one another on good shots and putts. The final score rarely matters (unless they tend to be serious golfers), as they are on the links to have a good time and get away from the stresses of everyday life.

Chapter 13: Final Thoughts

Golfing has become an incredibly popular sport. Most who participate say it's rather addictive, to say the least. But it's also a demanding sport. You'll quickly learn the differences between the seven iron and the seven wood, when to use the one iron (or that you'll likely never use it), and how to extract yourself from a sand trap. But the sport has tons of subtleties as well and the technical age has definitely made an impact. You can measure the "speed" of the course using a stimp meter and track your scores to establish your golf handicap using the latest software. You may even choose an interactive program to critique and help correct your swing.

From custom made golf clubs to the latest gadget, manufacturers of golf equipment and accessories have become a major economic industry. You'll find people who make a living giving golf lessons and schools that will take you in for a week or more to break those bad habits and help you establish a better stance and grip. It's more than being able to drive – it's about putting, getting in shape and keeping your eye on the ball. It is, very simply, golf.

The diversity of golf is found most obviously in the participants of golf. Any level of physically fit persons can choose golf as a sport. It is known to be beneficial exercise. Additionally, playing golf is good for getting out of the house and being outdoors. Golfers can enjoy the sun and wind note the beauty of the nature they're surrounded by, as the majority of courses are well landscaped and quite pleasing to the eye. Any societal level of persons can play golf. It is no longer the game of the rich and famous, on the contrary there are many affordable public golf courses emerging.

Whether you are male, female, young or mature, golf is a game of competitive spirit. We mustn't forget it is a patient competitive spirit. Not only are you competing against other golfers you are also being constantly challenged by difficult golf courses and weather conditions. The most appealing challenge for most golfers is the challenge of improving your game.

Lastly, golf is a game of honor. Surprised? Don't be. After all, golf is the only game where a person can call a penalty on themselves, and those who play with honor do. Of course, there are those players who claim to play golf, but wouldn't think of calling a penalty on anything they've done. Their scores are meaningless, and this kind of behavior will also show up in their day to day lives.

Remember ladies and gentlemen, a bad day on the golf course beats the best day a person can have at work.

Meet the Author

Larry Duncan grew up in Pasadena California and his love for the game of golf stems from his father. With hand me down clubs from his older brothers, Larry hit the golf course with his dad at the age of five. Larry's brothers became more interested in girls and cars rather than golfing with dad but Larry took advantage of this one-on-one time alone with his father.

Larry practiced, played every chance and fell in love with golf's challenges and sportsmanship. Larry played in Junior Leagues and tournaments and also played all four years on his high school golf team.

Larry continued to play recreationally in college while focusing on his education. Larry has enjoyed a career as a physical education teacher at a community college and teaches strength training and golf. When not teaching golf to students Larry loves to play and schedules weekend trips and vacations to courses on his bucket list.

www.ingramcontent.com/pod-product-compliance
Ingram Content Group UK Ltd.
Pitfield, Milton Keynes, MK11 3LW, UK
UKHW022120230426
12048UKWH00010BA/625